See No Evil

Diane Young

Orca currents

ORCA BOOK PUBLISHERS

Library and Archives Canada Cataloguing in Publication

Young, Diane
See No Evil / Diane Young.

(Orca currents)
ISBN 1-55143-664-7 (bound) ISBN 1-55143-619-1 (pbk.)

I. Title. II Series.

PS8647.093S44 2006   jC813'.6   C2006-903442-7

Summary: Shawn and Daniel witness a gang beating behind the local mall.

First published in the United States, 2006
Library of Congress Control Number: 2006928968

Orca Book Publishers gratefully acknowledges the support for its publishing
programs provided by the following agencies: the Government of Canada
through the Book Publishing Industry Development Program and the
Canada Council for the Arts, and the Province of British Columbia
through the BC Arts Council and the Book Publishing Tax Credit.

Cover design: Lynn O'Rourke
Cover photography: FotoSearch

Orca Book Publishers
PO Box 5626, Station B
Victoria, BC Canada
V8R 6S4

Orca Book Publishers
PO Box 468
Custer, WA USA
98240-0468

www.orcabook.com

Printed and bound in Canada

09 08 07 06 • 4 3 2 1

For Michael and Kate

chapter one

"All right. You can go. I would appreciate it, however, if you boys would make an effort to arrive on time in the future. Just once I would like to get through the first fifteen minutes of class without being interrupted by you two."

"Yes, ma'am," I mumble. As I get up from my desk, I can see Daniel making faces at me. He's crossing his eyes, letting his mouth droop open like he's a mental case.

"What's her problem?" he says as soon as Ms. Wolischuk leaves the room.

I just shrug and heave my knapsack over my shoulder. I can't wait to escape. We've been in detention for a whole hour just for being a few minutes late this morning.

"So, I didn't tell you," Daniel says as we trudge down the hall. "I went to Travis's party on Saturday night." Travis is a guy in our homeroom.

"Oh, yeah. Was it good?"

"Yeah, not bad. That new girl was there. You know which one I mean?"

I shake my head.

"Maya. You know who I'm talking about. She has long black hair."

"Oh, yeah," I say casually. "So what's she like?"

"Cool," Daniel says. "I think she likes you."

"Oh, yeah? Why do you say that?" I ask. The truth is, I'm thrilled.

"Well, she asked me a million questions about you."

A million questions? Wow. "She's okay," I tell him.

"Okay?" Daniel bumps my shoulder. "Okay? Get out of here, man! She's hot, and you know it!"

He's laughing, and I can't help grinning a bit too as we head outside. It's only five o'clock, but it's already dark. We cut across the yard toward the street, crunching leaves underfoot. I notice there is new graffiti scrawled over the school wall. It reappears just as fast as the janitors can clean it off. Gangs marking their territory.

When we get to the corner, the bus has just left. We could wait for another, but we decide to walk. Ignoring the red light, we cut across the road, dodging traffic.

Some storefronts are boarded up on this side of the street. Others have iron bars on the windows. After ten minutes or so, Daniel and I are nearly at the mall.

It's a busy place, even on a Monday. Cars are pulling in and out of the parking lot, and people are streaming through the front doors. Daniel and I aren't headed inside, though. We're strolling toward the service lane, behind the mall. If we hop over the fence, it's a quick shortcut to my apartment building and Daniel's house. We take this route home all the time.

On the fence, someone has scrawled a message in spray paint: See No Evil. It's good advice. As soon as we turn the corner, I know we've made a mistake. I hear someone swearing, then a thud and a groan. Daniel freezes, and so do I.

Down the lane, about thirty feet away, three guys are kicking someone who is curled up on the ground. One of them has an object in his hand, maybe a lead pipe. Is there a pool of something dark on the pavement, oozing around the person's head? I can't be sure. One of the lights in the lane is out, and it's hard to see. I'm paralyzed. I've stopped breathing.

Two of the figures are tall. The other one is short, but he seems to be in charge. I can't see their faces. They're all in black so they blend into the shadows.

I just stand there, listening to the blood

pounding in my head. I'm aware of Daniel beside me, can almost hear him breathing. We're dead quiet, but the gang must sense us. The short one has been crouching, looking at the person on the ground. Now he straightens up, turns in our direction. In a low voice, he says something I can't hear. For a second, he steps into the light, and I catch a glimpse of his face. It's angular and bony. Skull-like. I know who it belongs to. His name is Damien Sykes. Lots of people know him. I just pray he doesn't know me.

He's seen us. "Hey! You!" he shouts. Somehow his words break the spell, and we can move. Beside me, Daniel has finally found his feet. He slams into me as he wheels around and takes off in the same direction we've come from. I am right behind him. And then I'm ahead of him, because I'm taller and my legs are longer. And we're pounding back toward the parking lot, dodging honking cars and gasping for air.

"Run!" Daniel shouts as he catches up to me. I grab the handle of the door leading into the mall and yank it open, practically knocking down an old woman in the process.

"Hooligans!" she shouts after me, but I don't have time to stop. I am hurtling down the mall's main aisle, while shoppers either curse or stop and stare. I streak past the smaller shops toward the big discount store at the far end.

"Good evening!" the greeter says as I sprint through the doors. "Slow down, please," he calls after me.

But I don't slow down. Not until I am at the far end of the store, as far as I can get from danger and still stay indoors. I am walking up and down the men's underwear aisle, staring at packages of boxer shorts and sports socks. My heart is pounding while I try to drag air into my lungs.

Where's Daniel, I wonder. Did he follow me into the mall? The last thing I remember, he was telling me to run. I lost track of him after that. Could he still be outside? Did they catch him? I don't even want to think about it.

My lungs are begging for air. I bend over and try to catch my breath.

"You all right?" a middle-aged clerk asks me. "You need some help?"

"Ah, no. I'm fine," I gasp.

She nods, but doesn't look like she believes me. She retreats a few paces, keeping me in sight.

I pretend to be checking out men's underwear, but my mind is really back outside. I am remembering what I saw. The sales clerk must think I'm desperate to steal some socks because she's still watching me. I have finally calmed down a little, and I'm trying to decide what I should do next. That's when I hear the sirens outside. Someone must have called the police or an ambulance. The sales clerk forgets about me and wanders off to the window.

I choose that moment to turn around and head toward the exit. I push through the mall doors, and the cold air hits me like a slap. At the far end of the complex, I see an ambulance and a fire truck with their lights flashing. Heading in the opposite direction, I set off at a run, and I don't stop until I've reached home.

chapter two

"Where have you been?" Ethan asks in a whiny voice as soon as I step inside the apartment. "You were supposed to be home by four-thirty."

I kick off my shoes, adding them to the pile in the front hall. In the living room, my brother is sitting cross-legged in front of the TV, eating peanut butter out of the jar. He's dropped his knapsack beside him, but he's still wearing his winter jacket.

"Don't bug me," I say in a warning voice. I don't need attitude from a nine-year-old. Not right now.

"I'm going to tell Dad," he says. "You're supposed to come straight home and make me dinner." His brown eyes are big and glassy. I bet he's been watching TV for two hours straight.

"So I'll make dinner," I say, walking over to him. "Stop doing that. It's disgusting." I snatch the jar out of his hand and take it into the kitchen.

"But I'm hungry," he calls after me. A second later, he's glued to his program again.

In the kitchen, I put the peanut butter back in the cupboard. The room looks like the morning after a big party. The trashcan is overflowing; the sink is full of dishes. Ethan has added his own touches to the mess. He's spilled milk on the floor and upended a box of corn flakes all over the counter. Normally, I'd chew him out, but I'm not up to it right now. I'm thinking about what I just saw at the mall. You better concentrate, I tell myself. Just put it right out of your mind. I start cleaning up at top speed, sweeping the cereal back into the box and mopping up the milk.

I've got to feed Ethan quickly, I decide. Then convince him to shut up and not tell Dad I was late today. Dad gives me twenty-five dollars a week for looking after Ethan. I don't want to lose it. More important, I don't want any questions about why I was late. I open the fridge to see if there's anything for supper, but it's looking pretty empty. Let's hope there's macaroni and cheese, at least. I'm in luck. There's one box left in the cupboard.

I drum my fingers on the counter as I wait for the water to boil. My mind is darting around from one thing to another. What happened to the guy behind the mall? Was he badly hurt? I wonder suddenly if there is anything about it on the news.

"Hey, Ethan. Let me watch the TV for a second."

"That's not fair," he wails. "I'm watching my show."

"Brat," I mutter under my breath. He was never like this when Mom was around.

"Com'on, Ethan," I say, trying to convince him. "I won't be long."

"No!" he says, holding the channel changer behind his back. "I'm going to tell Dad you were late."

"Fine. You tell him I was late, and I'll tell him who broke the lamp." He doesn't say anything, but his forehead is all scrunched up like he's going to throw a tantrum—or cry. "Okay, forget it," I say, exasperated. I'll watch the news later.

In another ten minutes, the macaroni is finally ready. I heap it onto a plate and then hand it to him. He looks away from the screen for long enough to take the dish.

In the kitchen, I peer down at the shiny, orange mass left in the bottom of the pot. I've got a funny, clenching feeling in the pit of my stomach. I can tell that eating anything right now would be a bad idea. Instead I pick up the phone and dial Daniel's number. I really need to talk to him. But the phone rings four times, and then the answering machine kicks in. I leave him a message and then hang up.

A second later, I hear Dad's key in the lock.

"Why are all these shoes in the hall?" he asks as he walks in. He must be in a bad mood. Normally he doesn't notice how messy our apartment is.

I apologize. I don't want any arguments tonight. "I didn't expect you home so early," I tell him.

He walks into the kitchen, looks at the dishes in the sink. "Yeah, well, Riba cancelled. She had to work late." His face looks gray and tired under the kitchen lights.

He wanders into the living room, walks over to Ethan and ruffles his hair. "How you doing, kid?"

Ethan just nods, barely glances up at him.

"Ethan, how long have you been watching television?" Dad wants to know, but my brother doesn't answer.

"Right," Dad says. "That's enough. Take

that plate to the table. We're turning this thing off." And he does.

For a second, Ethan sits there, blinking. I can tell he's about to complain, then he looks up into Dad's face and seems to change his mind. He lets Dad lead him to the table.

"How's school?" Dad asks me.

"Yeah, everything's fine," I lie. I don't know why I say that, I just do. "I've got a lot of homework," I tell him. "I'm going to my room."

He's looking at his mail and just nods, without paying much attention to what I'm saying.

I head into the bedroom I share with Ethan, close the door, and stretch out on my bed.

Hours later, I'm still awake. The glowing numbers on the clock tell me it's two in the morning. The room is dark and shadowy, but if I try, I can make out Ethan's shape on the bed opposite me.

I must have slept a little, but it doesn't feel like it. I feel like I've been awake all night, watching the same loop of film over and over in my mind: Daniel and I turning the corner into the lane, three figures kicking someone who is on the ground, Damien looking up at me. Sometimes I think the guy on the ground is okay. I'm pretty sure I saw him move. At other times, I'm not so sure. Maybe he died. Maybe he's lying in the hospital right now, fighting for his life.

If he died, would that make us accessories to the crime? That phrase worries me. I've heard it before, but I'm not really sure what it means. I think it has something to do with witnessing a crime, but not doing anything about it. Not informing the police.

Is it too late to call them now? Maybe not. I could get up and sneak out to the kitchen and use the phone. But Dad might hear me. Besides, what would be the point? I heard the ambulance and the fire truck at the mall. The guy must be in a hospital now. The police must know what happened. Maybe they've already picked up Damien and the other guys.

Every time I close my eyes, Damien's face floats in front of me. It's a strange face, thin and bony. Could he see me clearly, I wonder. Maybe not. There was a light out in the lane, and it was dark where we were standing. But if he did see me, did he recognize me? Does he know who I am?

I don't think so, although he could probably find out. He used to go to my high school, but all I really know about him is what people say. Someone told me he was in a gang. I also heard he got expelled for beating up another student. I never knew whether to believe those things or not, but I always avoided him when I could.

In the bed across from me, Ethan turns over, kicks off the blankets, and mutters something. Is he waking up? I would really like to have someone to talk to, even my kid brother, but no, he's still fast asleep. I tried to reach Daniel three times last night before I finally gave up and stopped leaving messages. So now I don't even know for sure if he made it home safely. Suppose Damien caught him?

I worry about Daniel for a while, but I fall asleep eventually. The next thing I know, my father is telling me to get up, it's seven-thirty.

"Dad," I call out.

He comes back, stands in the bedroom door, a tall man in jeans and a flannel shirt, holding a cup of coffee. "What is it, Shawn?"

"I'm not feeling well," I tell him. I'm not really lying. I do feel sick. "I have a stomach ache. It kept me up last night."

Dad frowns. "That's too bad. Do you need to stay home?"

"I think so."

"You're not trying to skip a test?" he asks.

"No. I just don't feel well."

I'm in luck. Usually I have to be dying before Dad will let me take a day off school, but he seems to have other things on his mind. "Okay," he says. "Stay put. But Ethan, you need to get moving."

"I'm feeling sick, too!" my brother calls from under the blankets.

"Nice try," Dad says, heading back to the kitchen. "If you hurry up, Ethan, I'll give you a lift in the truck."

My brother finally sits up in bed, rubs his eyes. After a few seconds, he stands up and shuffles off to the bathroom. As he passes by, he looks down at me in bed. "I know you're faking," he says.

I stick my tongue out at him.

Half an hour later, they're gone, and I have the apartment to myself.

chapter three

By the time I arrive at school on Wednesday morning, I feel like I've dragged myself through heavy glue. I tried to talk Dad into letting me stay home again, but today he wasn't buying it. Now I really *do* feel sick. Of course that could just be the result of not sleeping well for two nights. I stayed inside all day yesterday, playing the guitar and watching TV. I kept thinking I'd see something about the attack on the news, but there was nothing. Sometimes I could almost believe it didn't happen.

Standing in front of my locker, I spin my combination, but the door is stuck. At first I can't get it open, then the moment I do, stuff starts sliding out like an avalanche making its way down a mountain—books, binders, papers, and eventually my basketball. I just stand there like a zombie as it bounces down the corridor.

"Hi, Shawn," a voice says from behind me.

I turn around. It's Maya. She gives me a little wave. I get a quick flash of her long, shiny black hair and wide smile before she disappears into our homeroom. It's obvious she's seen everything. Well, that figures. My timing has always been great.

Travis, whose locker is next to mine, dribbles the basketball back in my direction.

He's short and nerdy, no athlete. "So, where were you yesterday?" he asks. "Trying to skip the chemistry test?"

Oh, God. I forgot. After Monday night, it wasn't exactly at the top of my mind.

"Forgot," I admit. "What was it on?"

"Chemical reactions," he replies. "Don't worry. Everyone failed anyway."

I nod. "Yeah, well, I guess we'll all be going to summer school together," I tell him. Unless things change dramatically, I'll be lucky if I pass chemistry. Not to mention math. "What else did I miss?" I ask him.

Travis kicks his own locker door shut. "Special assembly. Cops came in, made a speech about gangs and violence. They said there'd been an attack behind the mall on Monday night. Do you know anyone named Amir? I can't remember his last name."

I shake my head, start stuffing books and binders back into my locker. I'm afraid to look at Travis in case my face gives something away.

Travis shrugs. "Me neither. The cops said he goes to West Gate," he says. "Anyway, the cops want anyone who saw what happened to call them." Travis suddenly laughs. "Guess they're on to you, Shawn."

I freeze. "What do you mean?" I ask him. My voice sounds high-pitched and weird— even to me.

Travis looks at me a little strangely. "Chill out, man. It was just a joke. Take it easy."

The bell goes, and we all straggle into Chemistry, which is homeroom. Looking around the class, I realize that Daniel is nowhere to be seen. "Hey, was Daniel at school yesterday?" I ask Travis.

He shakes his head. "No. I guess he decided to skip the test too."

That's really strange. I can't figure out why I haven't been able to reach him. When I called his house yesterday, no one answered. I decide to try him again today, over lunch.

As I slide into my seat, Maya flashes me another big smile. "Did you understand the homework?" she asks me.

"Homework? Did we have homework?"

She laughs. She seems to think I'm joking. I'm so out of it, I can barely manage a smile. "No, seriously," she says.

"I am being serious," I tell her. "I wasn't here yesterday. I didn't know we had homework."

"Oh." She turns away from me like she's puzzled or maybe she's just run out of things to say. I wish I could help her, but I can't. Not right now.

Ms. Wolischuk is handing back the marked tests. Occasionally she compliments someone, but mostly she just shakes her head. We're obviously a big disappointment to her.

When she comes to Travis, she says, "I wouldn't grin, if I were you," and slaps his test down on the desk. I can see 3 out of 20 in red pen at the top of the page.

I'm next in line. "Shawn, where were you yesterday?" she asks, stopping in front of me. She's a tall woman with short red hair and heavy designer glasses. For a split second, an image from one of Ethan's video games flashes before me—a dragon complete with red eyes and thick scales. Then it's gone. "Well? I'm waiting," she says.

"I was sick."

Her eyebrows shoot up so high they're practically in her scalp.

"I've got a note from my Dad," I say before she can ask any more questions.

A likely story, her face seems to reply. "I'll be expecting you at four o'clock today," she says ominously and then moves on.

"I think she's got the hots for you," Travis whispers, smirking.

I don't bother answering. I've got way too much on my mind, but Ms. Wolischuk turns around and fixes her gaze on Travis. "You can join your friend," she says to him. "Right here at four o'clock."

chapter four

After school, I head back to homeroom, ready to write my Chemistry test. Well, sort of ready. I crammed over lunch, in between wolfing down a sandwich and trying to reach Daniel. I don't know why he isn't picking up the phone.

When I reach Ms. Wolischuk's classroom, all the lights are out, and she is nowhere to be seen. Travis hasn't turned up, either. I hang around the hall for a while, wondering what to do. I'm not surprised about Travis—he likes to live dangerously—but it's totally unlike Ms. Wolischuk to forget about a test. At four-fifteen, I finally give up and head home.

Outside, the sky is still dark and threatening, and I zip up my jacket to keep warm. I decide to take the bus today so I can avoid cutting through the mall. Down at the corner, I stand inside the shelter to get out of the wind. Usually, there are a few other people to keep me company, but this afternoon I'm by myself.

For a while, I just stand there, watching the cars drive by. Then I start thinking about Daniel again. What's going on with him? He must have got home safely on Monday, I reason, or someone would have called to ask where he was. I know his mother has my number. Eventually, I get tired of puzzling over it and decide to listen to some music.

I set my knapsack down on the ground and dig out my Discman. I wish I had something new to listen to, but I don't have a lot of money to spend on music. Sometimes Daniel lends me a CD, and every once in a while, Mom sends me a couple of albums from Los Angeles. She has pretty cool taste in music. I miss her now that she's moved away.

When I was a kid and I had a problem, I'd always go to Mom. Dad isn't easy to talk to. He's always busy with something or other. Could I tell Mom what happened at the mall on Monday night? I consider calling her long distance and asking her what I should do. It would feel good to tell somebody about it, but I don't know. I might get her boyfriend Brad on the phone, and I really don't want to talk to him.

So I stand there in the shelter, staring off into space while I listen to a CD. At first I barely notice that someone is standing behind me. Then the person gets too close and nudges my shoulder. I turn, half-expecting it to be Travis or some other kid from my class, but it's Wendell Stewart.

"Wow. Wendell. I haven't seen you

for a long time." Wendell is the older brother of a friend of mine. Well, Cody used to be a friend until his family moved away last year. Daniel and I hung out with him a lot.

"So, bud. How you doing?" Wendell asks me.

"I'm okay," I tell him. "How 'bout you?" He's standing so close, we're practically face to face. I'd like to put some room between us, but there's nowhere to move. I'm right in the corner. At this range, I can see all the freckles on his face like they're under a magnifying glass.

He shrugs, looks around. "I've been busy, you know?" He pulls the hood of his black jacket up over his coppery hair, shifts back and forth from foot to foot like he's cold.

I nod. Wendell's an odd guy. I always liked Cody, but I never felt like I really knew Wendell. He always seemed to be in some kind of trouble at school. Then he dropped out.

"So, how's Cody?" I ask.

He shrugs. "He's okay, I guess. You know Cody. He's perfect, right?" His voice is edgy, sarcastic. I remember that Wendell is jealous of his brother. He thinks everyone prefers Cody for some reason, and maybe he's right. Cody was the easygoing one that teachers loved, while Wendell was the rebel.

"It's weird running into you like this," I tell him. "You don't live around here anymore, do you?"

He folds his arms across his chest. "I don't live too far away."

"I thought you moved."

"My old lady moved. Cody went with her. Not me."

I can't think how to respond to this, so I just kind of nod. I wish Wendell would step back and give me some space.

"So," he says. "It really sucks around here, doesn't it? I mean, it's so boring." He raises his eyebrows at me, inviting me to agree with him.

"Yeah, I guess so." What else can I say?

"Nothing to do, eh? Just go to school, go

home. Go to school, go home. And when you're not doing that, you got to look after your little brother, right?"

Look after my little brother? What made him say that? Before I can answer, he's shooting another question at me. "You still hang out at the mall?" I feel a prickling sensation running down my back.

"The mall?" I repeat, keeping my voice steady. "Yeah, I hang out there sometimes. Not much."

"Really?" He's looking at me like he doesn't believe a word I'm saying. "That's funny. I could have sworn I saw you there the other day. You and a friend."

"Oh, yeah?" I find myself sizing him up. Could I take him in a fight, I wonder. We're about the same height, but he's heavier than me. Probably tougher too.

"Yeah. You got a friend named Daniel, right?"

"Yeah, but we haven't been to the mall lately."

"Are you sure?"

I just nod. Why am I lying to him? I feel

like I've been threatened, but I'm not sure exactly how.

For a minute, Wendell doesn't say anything. Then he shrugs. "Hey. Guess I was wrong then." He extends his arm in front of me, leans on the shelter wall, deliberately blocking my path.

"The bus is really slow today," I say, abruptly changing the subject. "I wonder where it is?" Then I dart around Wendell like I'm faking a pass and slip out of the shelter. He probably thinks I'm nuts, but who cares? I feel safer out here. On the corner, I peer down the street, looking for the bus. It's two blocks away. Putting on my earphones, I pretend I'm engrossed in my music. Wendell is still standing in the shelter.

That's when things get bizarre. Because of the music, I don't hear him stroll up behind me. Without any warning, he suddenly yanks out my ear phone. What the—? I turn around and stare at him.

His face is inches away from mine. His eyes are narrowed. "Watch yourself, man. I wouldn't want you to get into any trouble. Know what I mean?" He hands the earphone back to me.

Before I can respond, the bus arrives, and the doors slide open. I shoot forward, taking the steps two at a time. I only turn to look back at Wendell once I'm safely inside. He's still there, leaning against the outside of the shelter, watching me. "See you around, Shawn Morrissey," he calls out. He's holding something in his hands, playing with it. It's hard to tell exactly what it is, but from where I'm standing, it looks like a knife.

chapter five

I turn the key and walk into our apartment.
The lights are out, and it is ominously quiet.

"Ethan?" I call.

There's no sign of my brother. It doesn't
look like he's home from school yet. I check
the time on the kitchen clock. It's nearly
five. He should be back by now.

I wander through the rooms, flicking on
lights. Dining room, living room, bedrooms,
bathroom. The apartment is empty. Back

in the kitchen, I stand still and think. Did Dad say Ethan was going to be late tonight? I don't think so.

Suddenly Wendell's words run through my mind. "Just go to school, go home. And when you're not doing that, you got to look after your little brother, right?" I feel the prickling sensation down my back again. Why would Wendell mention Ethan? My mind starts racing, coming up with crazy ideas. Would Wendell make Ethan a target? Kidnap him or something?

No. He's not that twisted.

Still, I'm not sure what to do. Ethan should be home by now. I tap my fingers on the kitchen counter and think. Ethan's best friend is Jamal. Maybe he knows something. Above the phone, Jamal's telephone number is copied in Ethan's large, round handwriting. We're not supposed to scribble on the wall, but it's a hard habit to break. I dial the number.

"Hey, Jamal. It's Shawn. Do you know where Ethan is?" I ask him.

"No." His voice is faint like he's on

the other side of the world, not just a block away.

"Well, did you walk home with him today?"

"Uh-huh."

Jamal is so shy I've never heard him utter a complete sentence. I've often wondered how he and Ethan communicate. Normally it doesn't matter, but right now I could use a little more information.

"Did Ethan say he was coming straight home?" I persist. "Jamal? Are you there?"

"Yes," he says at last. "I don't know where Ethan is," he adds in a whisper.

"Sure. Okay, Jamal." I thank him and hang up.

Well, that was odd. It was almost like Jamal knew something that he didn't want to tell me. So what should I do now? I decide to call Dad. When my father is working on a construction site, he sometimes leaves his cell phone in the truck. On those days, I can't reach him for hours. Today he picks up on the third ring. But just as I start explaining, there's a knock at the door. "Hold on," I tell him.

I go and peer through the peephole. Out in the hallway, Ethan is standing with his eyes crossed and his fingers stuck in his ears, presumably for my benefit. "Never mind," I tell Dad. "Everything's okay."

"Where have you been?" I practically explode.

Ethan ignores me. He kicks off his shoes and heads straight for the TV.

"Hey," I say, grabbing the back of his jacket. "Not so fast. Where were you?"

"Let go!" He shakes me off. "I was seeing my friend."

"Oh, yeah? Who's that?" I ask him. I catch hold of him again, but it's like trying to grip a cyclone. Finally I pin his arms behind his back. "Hurry up," I tell him. "I haven't got all day. Who were you seeing?"

"Matthew," he says. "He lives on the third floor."

I let him go. He has a friend on the third floor? That's news to me. "How'd you meet him?" I ask, but Ethan is already bored with the conversation. He's channel surfing on the TV. "Ethan?" I prompt him.

"What?"

"You're supposed to come straight home after school. Do you hear me? Otherwise I'm going to tell Dad." I put myself between him and the television screen. "Are you listening, Squirt?"

"Hey," he protests. "I can't see!"

"Did you hear what I said? You're not allowed to visit friends unless you get my permission first."

"Dad's the boss," he says, pushing me aside.

"Not when I'm minding you. When I'm minding you, I'm the boss. Right?"

He mutters something under his breath. I decide it's "yes."

"Good. So, what do you want for dinner tonight?" I ask him.

As usual he doesn't hear my question because he's hypnotized by the TV.

Dad has left some hamburger in the fridge. I take it out and find a can of tomatoes in the cupboard. Mom used to make chili all the time, but I can't remember what she did. I'll have to improvise.

While the meat is cooking in the frying pan, I decide to call Daniel again. On the third ring, his mother picks up the phone.

"Mrs. Cooper! It's Shawn. I've tried to call your house a million times over the last couple of days, but no one's answered."

"There was something wrong with the phone," she says. "Are you looking for Daniel?"

"Yes."

"I'm afraid he's sleeping."

Sleeping at six at night? I find that kind of hard to believe. "What's wrong with him?" I ask her.

"He has the flu," she tells me. "I'll get him to call you later, if he's better."

"Sure," I agree. I hang up the receiver. At least I know Daniel made it home safely Monday night. I'm willing to bet he hasn't got the flu, though. I decide to call him again later. I want to hear his version of Monday's events and tell him about my meeting with Wendell.

I've decided that running into Wendell

was definitely creepy. It was almost as if he was waiting for me. But why would he do that? And what was that business about seeing me at the mall? Was that just a coincidence, or was he also there on Monday night?

I turn our conversation over in my mind. Could Wendell be a member of Damien's gang? I really have nothing to link them together, except they both went to my school and they're about the same age.

The hamburger is almost done, so I empty a can of tomatoes into the pan. I sprinkle chili powder on the mixture and then taste it. It tastes like a spicy hamburger and tomatoes—which sort of figures. "Okay, Ethan," I call out. "Supper's ready." I begin dishing the chili into two bowls.

I take mine over to the table. Ethan is still glued to his show. I shrug. I'm just supposed to make his dinner, not spoon-feed him. If he doesn't want to eat, what can I do? A minute later, he gets up and goes to the kitchen. "What the heck is *this*?" he asks.

"Chili," I inform him.

"Coulda fooled me," he says. He carries his bowl carefully into the living room, puts it down on the floor in front of the TV. He's looking at it suspiciously. "And what's this?" he asks. With his fork, he fishes out a bit of tomato.

"What do you think it is? A meteorite?"

"It's a tomato, isn't it?" He puts his fork down. "That's it. I'm not eating it."

"Fine," I tell him. "Starve." I reach into my knapsack and dig out the novel I'm reading for English. I prop it open in front of me, but I can't concentrate.

After a few seconds, the phone rings. Thinking it's Daniel, I jump up and run to the kitchen to get it.

"Hello?" There's no response. "Hello?" I repeat. There's a click.

"Who was it?" Ethan wants to know.

"No one," I tell him. "They hung up."

"Yeah, that's happened before," he says. He turns back to the TV.

"When?" I ask him. "When did it happen?" But he's ignoring me again. "Was it yesterday, Ethan?" I persist.

"Yeah," he agrees. "Yesterday. When I got home from school. Somebody called, then they hung up."

I barely touch my supper after that. Do the telephone calls mean anything, I wonder. Is it just someone dialing the wrong number? Or could it be Wendell?

Suddenly it's the phone again. Startled, I jump up and grab it on the second ring. "Hello. Who's that?" My voice sounds aggressive, even to me.

"Take it easy," someone whispers. "It's me. Daniel."

"Daniel! I've called you a million times. What's going on?" I slide down the kitchen wall, sit there on the floor.

"Look, man, I have to be quick. My mom thinks I'm sleeping."

"Why are you pretending to be sick?" I ask him.

"I'm not pretending," he says in a low voice. "I really do feel sick."

"Did you tell anyone?" I ask him.

"No. Did you?"

"No. I stayed home from school yesterday, but my dad made me go today."

"What are people saying?"

I fill in the details for Daniel, but after a few minutes he interrupts me. "My mom's coming upstairs. I don't want her to hear this conversation."

"Look, we've got to get together and talk," I tell him. "Are you going to school tomorrow?"

"I don't know," he says. "Maybe we could meet tomorrow night at the arena. My mom is going out."

"The arena? Why there?" It's only five minutes away from Daniel's house, but it isn't close for me.

"Because no one will hear us. I don't want my sisters listening in."

"How can you go to the arena if they think you're sick?"

"I'll figure it out."

"I don't know if I can make it, Daniel."

"Just try. Meet me in the lobby at eight. Look, I've gotta go!" And with that, he hangs up.

I stand up, put the receiver back, and tap my fingers on the kitchen wall. How can I meet Daniel at the arena tomorrow night if I'm looking after Ethan? Dad flips out if I leave my brother alone for five minutes. And if Dad is home, it will be just as bad. He thinks I should stay in on weeknights and do homework, not hang out with my friends. Just what I need. Another problem.

chapter six

"Hey, I can't believe the Wolischuk let you off the hook with that lame excuse." Travis is kneeling beside me in the hall, transferring stuff from his knapsack to his locker. It's four, and everyone is heading home.

"It was true," I tell him. "I never got the message." It turns out that Ms. Wolischuk left a message for me on the blackboard yesterday. I was supposed to join her and

Travis in the detention room. That's why I couldn't find her.

"Yeah, right," Travis says, like I'm just making it all up.

Although we're friends, Travis has a way of getting under my skin. I decide to ignore him and focus on getting my books out of my locker and into my knapsack. I need to meet Ms. Wolischuk in homeroom. I can't concentrate, though, because Travis is still talking. "You know that guy who got beat up behind the mall Monday? Apparently he's still in the hospital. The cops were talking to some people in my apartment building yesterday. They think it was Damien Sykes's gang."

I just nod, keep pulling stuff out of my locker. I don't want to get into any conversations on this subject with Travis. He's got a big mouth. "I have Geography homework, and I can't find my binder," I mutter.

"Hey, Shawn."

Two white running shoes with bright orange laces are standing beside me. I look up and see Maya smiling down at me. I slowly straighten up. For one second, I'm standing inches away from her, looking into her wide brown eyes. Then she moves back a step.

"So. What's up?" I ask. She's kind of hovering, like she has something to say.

"Hey, did you take down those questions for English?" For some reason, she sounds kind of nervous.

"English? Oh, yeah. Somewhere." I look around me at the mess on the floor. "My English binder has to be here somewhere." I bend down, start to pick through the stuff at my feet.

I can sense Travis watching us with interest. I wish he'd get lost. He can be a real pain at times.

"You know what, Shawn?"

I look up at Maya. She's licking her lips like she's about to tackle an equation in algebra or maybe some really difficult gymnastic feat. "What?" I ask her.

"Would you have time to go for coffee? Maybe we could go over our homework."

Did I just miss something, or did Maya really ask me out? "Uh, sure. When were you thinking of?"

"Right now?" Her face is screwed up in a hopeful expression. "It would be so helpful. Really."

I catch a glimpse of Travis wiggling his eyebrows at me behind her back. What an idiot. "Sure," I tell her. "Let's go." As I stand up, I narrow my eyes at Travis, and he finally turns away. "I just need to grab my stuff."

I scoop up my textbooks and divide them between my locker and my knapsack. Then I lead the way through the crowded hall toward the side doors. When we hit the sidewalk, I can't believe it. It's still cold, but for the first time in days, the sun is shining.

As we stroll toward the coffee shop, I realize I can't think of anything to say. Suppose Maya can't think of anything, either? That's going to be embarrassing. As it turns out, though, silence isn't a problem. I hardly get to open my mouth. Maya keeps up a steady stream of conversation all the way to Coffee World.

"I hope I'm not talking too much," she says as we push through the restaurant doors. I shake my head. As far as I'm concerned, she can talk all she wants.

"I'm a little nervous," she explains.

I'd like to ask her why. It can't be me. I'm not the kind of guy who makes people nervous. At least, I don't think I am.

We stand in line and order drinks, and then find a table by the window. I'm all set to pull out our homework, but suddenly Maya doesn't seem worried about English anymore. Now she'd rather talk.

"So, have you heard the new album by Led Astray?" she asks me.

"Sure. It's great."

"The lead singer used to go to our school," she informs me.

"Yeah, I know."

"Well, we're going to see them tomorrow night. Would you like to come? They're at The Roxy. I think tickets are still available."

Wait a minute. Did Maya just ask me out

tomorrow? "Tomorrow night?" I stutter. "Uh, sure. I think I can go."

"Hey, that's great. So," she says, sipping her coffee. "Tell me about yourself."

"Oh. Uh–" I feel like I've been asked to stand up in class and make a speech. Suddenly I feel shy. "I don't know," I tell her, laughing a bit. "I live in an apartment over on Victoria Park with my dad and my little brother. We used to live in a house, but when my mom and dad broke up two years ago, we had to move. My best friend is Daniel. I play guitar in my spare time. Uh, I don't know what else to tell you."

"So your parents are divorced," she asks sympathetically. "That sucks, eh? Where's your mom?"

"She moved to Los Angeles with her boyfriend. He works for some sort of software company, and he got transferred there so she decided to go with him. Now I only see her like once or twice a year. What about you? Are your parents still together?"

Maya looks up at the ceiling and laughs. "Oh, yeah. You bet. They're together all right. They argue constantly, like all the time, but I can't imagine them living apart. They've been married for—oh, I don't know—since the seventies. My two sisters are a lot older than me. My mother had me when she was forty. She tells me I was an afterthought. They decided to have me to celebrate moving to Canada. I mean, go figure! Have you ever heard anything so weird?"

I have to agree. "That's pretty weird. So where did they move from?" I ask.

"Mumbai. It used to be called Bombay."

"Oh, yeah." I decide to look it up in an atlas. I ought to pay more attention in geography.

"That's in India," she says helpfully. "Have you ever been there?"

I shake my head. "I've never been out of the country. What about you? Have you been there?"

She nods. "Twice. I love it there. India is so beautiful."

To be honest, I'm hardly listening to what she's saying. I mean, I'm paying attention all right, but not really to the words. It's her lips that I'm focusing on. They're very pink and shiny. I start to imagine leaning forward and moving in for a kiss. I must be in a trance or something, because the next thing I know she's looking at me like she's waiting for an answer. "Are you okay?" she asks.

"Who? Me? Sure, I'm fine."

"That's good. Ready to go? Sorry to rush you, but I have to be home by five or my mother thinks I've been murdered or something. You know, I've really enjoyed talking to you, Shawn."

"Hey! Me, too." I guess I didn't hear her say it was time to go.

Slowly we stand up, zip our jackets and grab our knapsacks. Outside, the sun has dipped behind the buildings, and it's starting to get dark. We take our time strolling toward the corner.

"I go this way," she says, pointing in the opposite direction from my home.

I can feel myself starting to grin. "Hey, we never got to talk about English," I remind her.

"That's right! We never did. Oh, well. I'll figure it out." She gives me a big smile, and then turns to go. "Have a good night, Shawn. See you tomorrow morning in chemistry," she calls over her shoulder.

"Bye, Maya. See you tomorrow!" I'm waving goodbye when the word *chemistry* suddenly hits me like a punch. Chemistry! Omigod. I've missed writing my test for the second day in a row.

I check my watch. Ten to five. It's too late to go back to the school and find Ms. Wolischuk. I'll have to come up with a really good excuse tomorrow. Meanwhile, I have to go home and make Ethan's dinner. Then go meet Daniel.

chapter seven

The night is cold. By the time I reach the arena, I'm shivering and out of breath. The windows along the front of the building glow invitingly. Ahead of me, two fathers are lugging equipment bags while their kids trail behind them with their hockey sticks and skates. Ethan comes here to practice with his team. I used to play hockey here myself, before I quit a few years ago.

Inside the bright lobby, I rub my hands together to warm them and look around for Daniel. He's not here yet, but I'm early. The clock above the entrance reads five to eight. I find a place where I can stand comfortably and watch what's going on.

I'm worried about leaving Ethan at home alone. He wasn't happy that I was going out, and I had to bribe him not to tell Dad. I said he could play with his friend on the third floor again tomorrow if he promised to keep quiet. Dad won't be home until ten or ten-thirty, so everything should be fine.

While I'm waiting, I keep myself busy by looking at the photographs and hockey trophies in the glass cases. After ten minutes or so, I see Daniel pushing through the double doors. As he comes in, he stops for a second to look back outside.

"Hey." He barely makes eye contact with me before he starts looking around the lobby again.

"Are you okay?" I ask him. He has his hands buried deep in the pockets of his jacket, and he's rocking back and forth slightly, like he can't keep still.

"Yeah, yeah. I'm okay. It's just...I feel like I'm being followed or something." His dark skin gleams under the fluorescent lights. He has his toque pulled down low over his forehead, like some kind of disguise.

"Is that why you keep looking over your shoulder?" I ask him.

He nods. "When I turned the corner by my house, I noticed this guy standing in the phone booth. Maybe I'm imagining it, but I think he followed me here." He's licking his lips.

We both glance toward the wide windows and the parking lot outside. "Can you see him now?" I ask.

He shakes his head. "No. Maybe I'm wrong."

"Look," I tell him. "I've been thinking about this whole thing. We've got to talk to someone about what happened. You know, tell them what we saw."

A look of complete disbelief crosses his face. "Are you kidding me? You've got to be crazy! We can't tell *anyone*."

"No, I think we have to," I persist. "The guy who got beat up is still in the hospital. We have to tell somebody."

"Who? The cops? You want to tell the cops? Are you out of your mind?"

Daniel has started to raise his voice, and a man glances at us as he walks by.

"Keep it down," I warn him.

He moves a little closer to me and lowers his voice a notch. "Did you see who that was on Monday night? Because I did. It was Damien Sykes."

"I know," I tell him quietly. "I saw him too."

"Well, then?" Daniel says, as though his point should be obvious. "Do you want to be next? You know what he's like. If he finds out we've been talking to the cops, we'll wind up like that guy in the hospital."

I sigh and run my hand through my hair. I was hoping Daniel would agree that going to the police was the right thing to do. Keeping this to myself is making me feel sick.

"What about our parents?" I suggest. "Suppose we told them?"

"No way. You tell your dad or I tell my mom and we might as well go to the police. No way." He sets his jaw, folds his arms across his chest.

"Okay," I say reluctantly. I can see I'm not going to change his mind. "Look, something kind of weird happened to me yesterday. I don't know if it means anything, but I ran into Wendell Stewart." I tell Daniel what happened at the bus stop.

Daniel shakes his head. "That *is* freaky. Do you think he's part of Damien's gang? Could he have seen us at the mall?"

"I don't know."

"Something else is creeping me out," Daniel says. "I can't find my ID."

I'm so focused on what happened on Monday night, that it takes me a minute to understand what he's saying. "Your ID," I repeat.

"Yeah, you know. My student card. With my picture on it."

Why is he worrying about his ID at a time like this, I wonder. "So what's the big deal?" I ask him. "Go to the office and ask for another one."

"You don't get it," he says impatiently.

"Well, what?" I ask. I'm mystified.

"The last time I had the card was Monday. I think I might have dropped it." He waits for his words to sink in.

"You mean—at the mall?" I ask incredulously. How is that possible? "No way," I tell him. That would be unbelievably bad luck.

He just nods.

"Look," I reason with him. "You could have dropped the card anywhere. How likely is it that you dropped it in the lane? You probably dropped it on the street somewhere."

Daniel is shaking his head. "It was in my jacket pocket with my money. I remember feeling something drop when we were running. You know, after we saw—" his voice starts to crack. "I didn't want to stop to find out what it was."

I just stand there staring at him for a minute. If Daniel dropped his ID card in the lane, he could be in real danger. It all depends on who found it. "Look," I finally say, "have you been back to see if the card's still there?"

"Are you kidding?"

"You have to look for it. Go tomorrow, during the day. Maybe it's still on the ground. I mean, how likely is it that Damien found your ID on Monday night? It was dark." I almost believe what I'm saying myself.

Daniel shrugs. "Maybe," he finally says. He shakes his head. "This thing is really getting to me."

I know what he means. We zip up our jackets and head out into the darkness. Overhead the full moon is a gold disc hanging low in the night sky. We head toward the park, zigzagging around the cars in the outdoor lot. From this point, it's only five minutes to the street.

We're near the edge of the parking lot when something makes me turn my head. I freeze for a second, trying to see who or what it is. Beside me, Daniel has also stopped. "What do you hear?" he asks in a low voice.

"Over there," I hiss. "Behind the black van." I can't see him now, but a second ago I caught a glimpse of a figure in a black sweatshirt. I'm sure of it. He's stepped behind the vehicle, hiding from view.

Daniel turns his head slightly to look. "It's him! Run! We've gotta get out of here!" Daniel breaks into a sprint, heading across the dark stretch of grass, toward the bright streetlights and passing cars.

Suddenly I feel like I have an electric current running through me. Before I know it, I'm pounding after him, feeling my heart thumping in my chest. Once again we're running away, too afraid to look behind us.

By the time we reach the street, we're gasping for breath. Daniel doesn't say a word, just turns and keeps sprinting toward his home. Now that I'm on the sidewalk, I pause for a second and glance behind me. I'm sure the person is still there in the park, ten or twenty feet back, in the shadows. I'm not going to stick around to find out, though. I start jogging in the direction of my building. By the time I've reached the lobby, I've slowed to a fast walk. As I push through the front door, I look over my shoulder once again. There's no one in sight.

As I ride the elevator, my breathing slowly returns to normal. I have no idea who I saw in the parking lot or even if the person was a threat. I just know that something about him gave me a bad feeling.

As I put the key in the lock, I glance down at my wristwatch. Twenty minutes after nine. Not too late. I should be okay. Should be—but I'm not. As I push open the door and walk in, I see my father standing in the kitchen with his hands on his hips.

For a split second, I freeze. Neither one of us says anything. Finally I break the silence. "You're home early," I observe.

"Yes, I am," my father agrees. "Come on in, Shawn. Don't just stand there. You and I need to have a little talk."

chapter eight

When I arrive at school on Friday morning, I find Daniel waiting for me beside my locker. It's the first time he's been back since Monday.

"Hey, that was weird last night. I saw that guy standing beside the van, and I just got a really bad vibe from him. Sorry if I scared you," I tell him.

Daniel is shaking his head. "Never mind that," he says. "Something's happened."

I look at him curiously. "What's up?"

Behind him, I can see Travis eavesdropping as he shoves books into his locker. The guy has big ears. Why is he always so interested in our business?

"When I got home last night, the cops were there," Daniel says in a low voice.

"No way! At your house? Why?" My mind immediately starts dreaming up all kinds of reasons.

"Someone turned in my ID card yesterday."

"So that's good," I tell him. "At least Damien hasn't got it."

Daniel shakes his head. "I don't know about that. The cops asked me a lot of questions. They got my mom all upset."

"What did they ask you?"

"They wanted to know how I lost the card."

I shrug. "How does anyone lose anything? Did you tell them it fell out of your pocket?"

"Yeah, but they wanted to know when I was in the lane at the mall and what I was doing there. Apparently someone found my card on Tuesday morning. They just didn't bother to turn it in until yesterday."

"So what did you tell the police?" I ask him.

Daniel looks unhappy. "I don't know. I mostly told them the truth. I said I took a shortcut home from school on Monday afternoon and that's when I lost it. But they wanted to know the time."

I'm beginning to see Daniel's problem. "And what did you say?"

"I said I wasn't sure. Then they asked me to try to remember, and I said it might have been four-thirty."

We stare at each other. Both of us know it was later than that.

"I think the cops believe I was involved," he finally blurts out. His voice is starting to crack.

"Hey, take it easy," I tell him.

Travis has stopped piling stuff in his locker and is openly staring at us now. "Hey, Travis," I say to him. "Can you hear everything, or should we speak up?"

His face goes bright red, and he slams his locker shut. Then he saunters off. I didn't think it was possible to embarrass Travis.

I turn my attention back to Daniel. "Look, we didn't do anything wrong, okay? Why are you feeling so guilty?"

"I don't know," he says. His voice sounds shaky. "I guess I'm thinking we should have told the police what we saw."

"Okay," I agree, taking a deep breath. "We can still do that," I tell him. But before I can say any more, the bell sounds, and seconds later the National Anthem starts. We stand there, waiting for it to finish. Great. Once again, we're late for chemistry.

Mentally, I am preparing myself for the wrath of Ms. Wolischuk, but for once I'm in luck. She has finally decided to take a day off. In her place, we have a scrawny substitute teacher who looks barely older than us. He seems to be having trouble finding the class list and ignores us as we slip into the room and take our places.

After class, Daniel goes one way and I

go another. When I return to my locker at noon, he's nowhere to be seen.

"Daniel has to write a make-up test over lunch," Travis informs me. "Don't bother waiting for him. Going to the caf?"

I nod, and he falls into step beside me.

"So, is Daniel in some kind of trouble or something?" he asks.

"What do you mean?"

"Well, I heard him talking about the police."

MYOB, I think to myself. Out loud, all I say is, "It's nothing," and change the subject.

A minute later, Maya comes out of the cafeteria with her friends Cali and Denise on either side of her. When she sees me, she breaks into a wide smile. "Hey, Shawn! I was looking for you."

I can tell I'm starting to grin.

"So I had fun yesterday," she says. She seems to have lost her shyness.

"Yeah. Me too." We hover for a second, just staring at each other. Okay, now it's my turn to say something. Over Maya's shoulder, I can see Cali and Denise checking me out. I wish I could think of something clever to say. For some reason, I'm always tongue-tied when Maya's around.

"So, are we still on for tonight?" she finally asks.

"Tonight," I repeat. I try to remember what's happening tonight.

"You know," she says. Her forehead is starting to wrinkle as she looks at me. "I thought you wanted to see Led Astray."

"Right!" Crap. How could I forget I said I wanted to see them? But I can't go anywhere tonight. Dad grounded me for leaving Ethan alone yesterday.

"You *do* want to see them, don't you?" Maya asks me. I can tell by her expression that she's getting upset.

"Uh, yeah. I really do. But—ah, I can't." Did that make any sense?

"I don't understand," she says.

I take a deep breath. "I'm really sorry, Maya, but I can't go out tonight."

Her nostrils flare, and sparks practically

fly out of her eyes. "You can't!" she repeats.

"No. Look, I'm sorry," I tell her.

"No, you're not! Oh, whatever," she says. And with that, she spins around and stamps off. Cali and Denise give me one last pitying look before they turn around and follow her.

A second later, Travis slaps me on the back. "Congratulations, Shawn," he says. "I think that went really well."

chapter nine

"How come you're home?" I ask Dad. For some reason, my father is standing in the kitchen at six o'clock on a Friday night. "Don't you usually see Riba on Fridays?"

He's flipping through the Yellow Pages. "Riba and I broke up," he says.

Wow. I'm surprised to hear that. Dad's been going out with Riba for six months now. I thought they were pretty happy together. "Hey, I'm sorry," I tell him.

Dad shrugs. "That's okay," is all he says.

I'd like to ask him what the problem was, but I bet he won't tell me. Dad's not a big talker. I'm not even sure why he and Mom broke up. When I once asked if she left him for Brad, he just said it wasn't like that.

"You haven't forgotten you're grounded, have you?" he asks me.

I shake my head.

"Well, since we're all going to be home together, should we order a pizza?" He has the telephone book open to Restaurants.

"Yes!" Ethan shouts from the living room. "I'd like pizza!"

By eight o'clock, the three of us are sitting on the sofa, watching a sitcom. The empty pizza box is lying open on the floor. I'm trying to concentrate on the show, but my mind keeps wandering. Then I look over at Dad and see he's fallen asleep. I decide it's a good time to call Daniel.

"Did the police call you again?" I ask him in a low voice.

"No. I mean there's no reason for them

to call me, right?" He sounds calmer than he did this morning.

"Right."

"I'm still worried that they suspect me, though. They just don't have any proof."

"That's why we've got to tell them the truth," I argue. "I was thinking, there's something called the Crimeline. People call it and leave tips. What about that? We don't have to leave our names or anything."

"Yeah, but the police can still trace the call."

"Well, we could call them from a pay phone."

"Maybe."

"Look, let's talk tomorrow morning. We can go to a phone booth together and make the call."

He agrees, and I promise to call him around eleven. But when I wake up the next morning, it's almost noon. Dad and Ethan must be at hockey practice because the apartment is silent. For a few seconds, I think about turning over and going back to sleep. Then I remember my conversation with Daniel and change my mind. I get up and shuffle off to the kitchen. As usual, the sink is full of dishes waiting to be washed. I open the cupboard doors, searching for something to eat, but all I can find are corn flakes.

Wandering into the living room, I step over the pizza box still lying on the floor from last night. Watching TV with my dad and little brother wasn't much of a punishment. To be honest, I don't really blame Dad for grounding me. We had a deal, and I broke it, so he had to do something. That's fair.

I start thinking about Dad and Riba and that makes me think about Maya. I wonder if she went to see Led Astray with her friends last night. She probably hates me now, but what can I do? It occurs to me that I never told her I was grounded. Maybe she would have been more sympathetic if she had known why I bailed. I mean, Daniel would understand if I cancelled because I was grounded. He wouldn't hold it against me.

I look over at the kitchen clock. It's twelve-thirty. I should really call Daniel. Picking up the phone, I dial his number.

"So, do you still want to make that call?" I ask him.

He sighs. "I guess so. I have to help my mom do some stuff first. Then I have a pile of homework. The vice-principal called to say I'm way behind because I was absent all week."

"Fine. Call me when you're ready." I spend the day watching TV and playing guitar. I even open up my math textbook and do the first three questions. Soon it's four o'clock, and Dad and Ethan are back home. I decide it's time to try Daniel again.

"Are you ready?" I ask.

"After supper," he tells me. "We can phone from the mall."

"The mall? Are you sure you want to go there again?" I ask him.

"I can handle it if you can," he says.

"Okay," I agree reluctantly. "See you at seven. In front of the discount store."

chapter ten

By the time I reach the mall, it's dark. It was about this time of day that Daniel and I were here on Monday. At the thought, my stomach starts flip-flopping, and I consider going home. Then, ignoring the feeling in my gut, I push through the front doors.

There are still lots of people milling around and shopping, even on a Saturday night. I wind through the crowds, heading toward the far end where we've arranged to meet. It's already seven, but Daniel is nowhere in sight. Finding a place to stand that's out of the way, I wait for him. After a while, though, it's nearly seven-thirty, and I'm starting to wonder why he's so late.

On the wall opposite me is a row of pay phones. I go over to one and call Daniel's house. I get his sister Keneesha.

"Daniel left a long time ago," she says. "He should be there by now."

Puzzled, I thank her and hang up. Where could he be? It only takes ten minutes to walk here from Daniel's house. I look around me. Maybe he's killing time in the music store. Sometimes we come here on Saturdays to listen to new CDs. I head inside. I wander from one end of the store to the other, checking out new releases as I go, but there's no sign of him. A few minutes later, I'm back outside, looking around.

Could he be in the arcade? When we were younger, we used to go there a lot to play video games. Inside, the space is dimly lit, and it takes a minute for my eyes to adjust to the light. Several rows of machines offer games like Alien Invasion and X-Treme Car Chase. The players are mostly boys Ethan's age. Every once in a while, though, I see an adult. I don't think I've ever noticed how creepy this place is. Still, there's no sign of Daniel.

Wandering back out to the mall, I stand there for a few minutes, scanning the crowd. In the end, it isn't Daniel I see. At least not right away. The person I see first is Wendell, standing near the back exit. Even though the hood of his sweatshirt is up, I can tell it's him from a bit of copper-red hair that's sticking out. He is deep in conversation with someone. I shift position to get a better look, and then I wish I hadn't. Even at this distance, I can easily see it's Daniel.

I stand there, feeling stunned. What's Wendell doing here? And why is Daniel talking to him? As I try to decide what to do, another figure emerges from the crowd just ahead of me. I'm not sure why I notice him because he's not the sort of person who would normally stand out. He's short and dressed all in black. What makes him distinctive is his face. It's bony, almost skull-like. Damien Sykes. I feel frozen as I watch him stroll in the direction of Daniel and Wendell as though he has all the time in the world.

When he arrives, they both turn toward him. There's no surprise on Wendell's face. He just nods and says something. But Daniel's expression is a different story. Even from here, I can see the look of shock. Then everything suddenly speeds up. I watch Damien and Wendell begin edging Daniel toward the exit. "Shout!" I want to tell him. But Daniel doesn't say a word. In a second, the three of them are out the back doors, swallowed by the darkness. Finally I understand what's going on.

Spinning around, I start running toward the opposite end of the mall where the security office is located. As I run, I look around for a guard. Usually there are at least two people on patrol, but today I can't find them.

"Hey, watch out! Where do you think you are?" someone shouts at me as I bump into him.

I don't have time to reply. I keep jogging toward the office, hoping I will find one of the guards before I get there. At last, I arrive, out of breath. In front of me, two middle-aged men are sitting in their shirtsleeves, drinking coffee and laughing.

"Quick! There's a fight," I tell them.

Suddenly, they're all action. Both men jump to their feet, grabbing their jackets and their telephones. "Where?" one of them asks.

"Behind the mall. Two guys have taken my friend outside."

"At which end?" he asks. The other security guard is already on the phone, calling for help.

"Near the discount store."

The two men break into a run. I follow them down a corridor and through an exit I've never noticed before. Suddenly we're outside the mall, in the back lane.

To my left, the guards are already

pounding toward the other end of the lane. There, under the cold glare of the overhead lamps, are two figures. I can only see their outlines, but I know who they are.

Someone shouts, "Run!" and for a few seconds, it's hard to see what's happening. Damien and Wendell tear off in opposite directions, but so do the guards. Then everyone seems to vanish, and it's very still.

For a second, I just stand and stare. And then I force myself to walk over to Daniel and kneel down where he's lying curled up on the ground.

"It's me. Shawn," I tell him. He has his arms clamped around his head and won't move. "It's okay," I assure him. "It's okay."

I can see now that he's shaking. He stays curled up like that for the longest time. After a while, the guards come back, and then the ambulance and police turn up.

chapter eleven

By the time the ambulance has gone, and everyone is back in the security office, it's nearly nine. I'm tired, and I'd like to go home.

"Do you need me anymore?" I ask one of the police officers. There are only two of them left. One is a young woman. The other is an older man.

"No. You can go," the woman says. "We have your address if we need any more information from you."

"Thanks." I can't get away quickly enough. Outside the mall, I take a deep gulp of cold air. The parking lot is still busy. It's like nothing has happened. The ambulance has taken Daniel to a hospital, but I don't know if he will be okay. The police caught Damien. I saw two officers handcuffing him and forcing him into a patrol car. One of the guards told me that the other guy escaped. That must be Wendell.

As I walk along the street toward my building, I start feeling shaky. Soon, it's getting worse with each step. What's wrong with me? I'm feeling really bizarre, almost like I can't breathe. I just want to be safely at home. I want to be inside my apartment with the door locked and chained.

I speed up my pace. I'm walking so quickly my lungs are starting to burn, but I don't care. I'm nearly there. And then I'm turning into the circular driveway outside my building, almost running for the doors. An older man pushes through the entrance just as I get there. He glances at me curiously but keeps on walking.

Before I go inside, I turn and look over my shoulder. Everything seems normal. The man I just passed is heading toward the bus stop on the corner. Cars are driving back and forth the way they always do on the busy street outside my building. When I look up at the night sky, I can see a bank of high, dark clouds. The moon and stars are hidden.

I should feel relieved once I'm inside the brightly lit lobby, but for some reason, I don't. I look around me. Usually someone else is around, but tonight the lobby is deserted. I press the button and wait for the elevator. When it arrives at last, I get on and push the ninth floor.

As the doors start to slide shut, I exhale and relax. And then, at just that moment, someone inserts an arm between the two doors and pushes his way on. The person is about my height. He's dressed in a black hooded sweatshirt that hides part of his face.

For a split second, I hesitate, and that's all the time he needs. It happens so quickly

I hardly have time to understand what's going on. There's an arm around my neck, and I feel like I'm choking.

"So what did you tell the cops?" he asks. He's standing behind me, but I don't have to see his face to know that it's Wendell. I recognize his voice.

"Nothing." My own voice is hoarse, scared. "I didn't tell them anything." Obviously, it's the only possible answer.

Wendell jerks his arm tighter around my throat, and things start to go black in front of me. Far away, I can hear him saying, "I don't have time for games. I know you spoke to the cops. What did you tell them?"

"Nothing!"

"Did you give them my name?"

I would answer him, but I can't. I'm going to pass out, I can tell. And then the elevator suddenly jolts to a stop, and the doors slide open at my floor. For a second, Wendell loosens his grip on me, and I can breathe. The oxygen is like an electric shock. Somehow I rip away from him, and then I'm in the hallway, running. I have no idea which direction I'm going.

A second later, I feel him grabbing the back of my jacket. We fall to the ground and roll around there. "What did you tell the police?" he asks again.

"Nothing!" He's sitting on my chest.

"Do you want to die?"

Somehow I manage to heave him off me, then something that feels like a brick hits me in the face, and my eyes begin to water. I kick back at him, and he lets go of me in surprise. I struggle to my feet again and stumble down the hall.

Ahead of me, at the far end, I can see the fire escape door. That's where I'm headed. Maybe I should have a plan, but the truth is, I don't. I'm just thinking, "Get out!"

I dive through the door. The fire escape is dimly lit, and the concrete stairs are steep. I take them two at a time. A second later, Wendell comes crashing through the door, only he misses the stairs completely. He sort of dives down them, head first. I turn in time to see him hit the landing.

When people do that in the movies, they spring right up again, but Wendell just stays where he is. His head and body are on the landing, his legs are pointing up the stairs. I'm standing below him, still poised to run, but I stop for a second. I don't know why. Maybe I think he's killed himself, or maybe I'm just curious.

He doesn't move for the longest time. Then he finally struggles to sit up. "What's the matter with you?" he says roughly.

I don't say anything, just stand there, staring up at him. I can see blood oozing from a gash on his forehead. I hesitate for a second longer, wondering what I should do.

"Go on," he says. He gestures toward the fire escape. "Run! I know where to find you!"

I don't wait any longer. A moment later, I'm through the fire escape door and into the eighth floor hallway.

chapter twelve

"What's wrong?" Dad asks me.

"Nothing," I lie. I'm sitting at the dining room table, staring out the window. In my mind, I'm still going over last night's events and trying to figure out what to do next. So far I haven't got any answers.

"It's one o'clock," Dad says. "You've been sitting there for a long time."

I can tell he's staring at my back, but I decide to ignore him. I haven't said a word about yesterday. When I finally made it safely back to the apartment, Dad and Ethan were out at a hockey game. I went to bed, planning to lie awake and listen, in case Wendell came back. Instead I fell asleep almost instantly and barely heard Dad and Ethan when they got home.

Dad walks around the table so he can look at my face. "Are you sure you're okay?" he asks me. "It looks like you've done something to your eye."

"It's nothing," I tell him. In fact, I have a bruise on the right side of my face, where Wendell hit me. Last night I was afraid it would turn black, but it's not too noticeable this morning.

"Did you get into a fight yesterday?" he probes.

I glance up at him. He's looking at me curiously with his arms folded across his chest. Even though it's a Sunday, he's wearing the same jeans and work shirt he wears all week. He's not much of a dresser, I find myself thinking. Maybe that's why Riba dumped him. He knows something is up with me, though. I can tell. Should I share last night's events with him? I'm worried that if I tell him too much, he will call the police. I choose my words carefully.

"Something happened at the mall yesterday. I was asleep when you got home last night so I didn't get a chance to tell you."

"What was that?" he asks.

"Some guys attacked Daniel."

Dad's face registers shock. "You're kidding! Is he all right?"

"I don't know. An ambulance took him to the hospital. When I called his house last night, no one answered."

Dad sits down opposite me at the table. "Who attacked him?"

I shrug. "Just some guys. They're members of a gang. Daniel got on the wrong side of them, and they decided to get even. When I saw what was happening, I called the security guards."

Dad's brows knit together as he tries to make sense of it. I can see Ethan look over at us from the television where he's playing a video game. "So what happened when the police turned up?" Dad asks.

"They arrested one of the guys. The other one got away."

Dad is giving me that look, like he thinks there's more to the story, but I'm not sure I want to share any more than this. Wendell told me to keep my mouth shut. If I tell Dad and he calls the police, Wendell will come back for me for sure. I stand up and say, "I'm going to call Daniel's house again. I want to know how he is." I head toward the phone in the kitchen, ignoring Dad's look.

Before I can dial Daniel's number, though, there's a knock at our door.

"Who's that?" my father wonders. It's unusual for anyone to come up without first buzzing us from the intercom downstairs.

I shrug, wander over to the door and look through the peephole. The young woman standing there has chin-length black hair and a calm, pleasant face. It's distorted by the glass, but there's no mistaking her. It's the police officer who was at the mall yesterday.

"Who is it?" Dad asks again, coming to the door. I move aside. He takes a look and then opens up.

"Good afternoon, sir," the woman says. "I'm Constable Chen. I'm looking for Shawn Morrissey. Oh, there you are!" she says, noticing me behind Dad. "May I come in?"

Dad steps aside, shows her into the living room. Ethan has stopped playing his game and is staring at us with his mouth hanging open.

"Would you like a seat?" my father asks her. He clears away Ethan's homework and some of the newspapers lying on the sofa and motions for her to sit down.

"Thank you," she says. She perches on the edge of the couch like she's afraid of it, and to be honest you can't really blame her. Our living room is a mess. She turns to face Dad. "Did your son tell you what happened yesterday at the mall?" she asks.

"Yes. Just a moment ago, in fact."

She gives me a friendly smile. "I'm sure you're proud of him."

I want to say, "Wait a minute, you don't know the whole story," but Constable Chen is already pushing on. "I just wanted to go over some details with you, Shawn, to make sure we've got all the facts down right. Is that okay?"

All I can do is nod. I'm nervous about what she's going to ask me, but she starts off with things like the spelling of my last name and my telephone number.

Then she asks, "So Shawn, when did you see Daniel leave the mall?"

I think back. "I guess it was about seven-thirty."

She writes this down in a notebook. "Okay. Now, I'd like you to tell me exactly what happened."

I stare at my hands. I'd like to be honest, because that would help her catch Wendell. After what he and Damien did to Daniel, I don't care what happens to *them*. But how can I tell her the story without getting into trouble myself? If Wendell finds out I've tipped off the police, he'll kill me. Finally I decide to tell her what I saw without mentioning any names.

"So Daniel left the mall with two males at about seven-thirty. Is that correct?"

I agree, and she writes it down. Then she asks, "Would you be able to recognize these two people if you saw them again?"

I'm starting to feel sick. I'd like to tell her I don't want to answer any more questions. Instead I say truthfully, "Yes, I think so."

I'm waiting for her to ask me if I know their names, but she only says, "That's great. Now, Shawn, I'd like to show you some photos and see if you recognize anyone."

"Right now?" I ask, startled. I was counting on having some time to think everything through.

"I've brought the photos with me," she says. She has her head tilted to one side like she's trying to read my mind.

What can I say? I'm trapped. I've already told her I got a good look at the two suspects. Should I pretend I don't recognize them now?

"Shawn?" Dad prompts me. He's looking at me with a frown, trying to figure out what's wrong.

There's no way to get out of it. "Okay," I agree reluctantly.

Constable Chen takes a binder out of her bag and places it on the coffee table. "I'm going to select eight shots for you to look at. I'd like you to stop me if you see anyone you recognize."

She begins laying down photos of people's faces. They're all guys who are about Wendell's age. I've never seen the first three people. The fourth one is Damien.

I take a deep breath. "Yeah, that's one of them," I tell her.

"Good," she says. "Now, I just have a few more I'd like you to look at." She places the photos down, one after another, like she's dealing a hand of cards. The very last shot is Wendell. His head is shaved in the picture, but it's definitely him.

"Take your time," she tells me.

I hardly hear her. Inside my head, I'm having a conversation. A voice is saying, if Wendell learns you've identified him, it's all over. He's going to come after you and you'll wind up just like Daniel. But he may come after me, anyway, I reason. He never promised he wouldn't be waiting for me after school tomorrow.

I look up from the picture. "That's the other one," I say, pointing to Wendell's photo.

"Good," she says. "That's very good."

"Tell me, is Shawn in any danger?" Dad asks suddenly.

Constable Chen has been taking down notes. Now she looks up at my father and then over at me. "I don't think your son is in any immediate danger," she says, speaking carefully.

"And why is that?" Dad asks.

She lays her pen and notebook down. "Because we have both suspects in custody."

"You've got both of them?" I ask in surprise. "The guard told me you only caught one person."

"At first. We picked up the second suspect late last night."

"So you arrested the other guy last night?" I ask. "This one?" I say, pointing at the picture of Wendell. I'm staring at her now, trying to put it all together.

"That's right," she says. "Just around the corner from here, as a matter of fact."

Is it possible that I'm safe, after all? Constable Chen and my father are discussing something, but I've stopped listening to them. I have only one thought in my mind. The police have arrested Wendell.

"So, that's it!" Constable Chen says. Gathering up her things, she stands up and extends her hand to Dad. "By the way," she says, pausing at the door. "This morning, I called the hospital to ask about your friend. He's going to be fine."

"Daniel? He's going to be okay?" It's the best news I've heard all week.

She just nods. "He'll need a bit of time, but he'll get better fast. And Shawn?" she says.

"Yes?" I ask, looking up. I'm still sitting on the sofa, feeling a little dazed.

"Thanks again for your help! I mean it," she says, giving me a smile. A moment later, she's gone.

Is it really over? I can't believe it. I feel like someone who has just stepped off a spinning ride. Dad wanders back into the living room and stands there with his arms folded across his chest, just looking at me.

"What?" I ask him.

He sighs. "I don't suppose you're going to tell me the whole story now?"

"What do you mean?"

Dad just shakes his head. "Fine, okay," he says. He knows he's got as much information out of me as he's going to get. "So what do you guys feel like doing?" he asks, changing the subject. "It's Sunday afternoon. We should make the most of it. How about a pickup game at the arena?"

"Yeah!" Ethan shouts. "That's a good idea. Let's go!"

Do I want to spend Sunday afternoon playing hockey with my Dad and kid brother? I look out the window for a second. For the first time in a week, I feel free, almost light-headed. There are lots of things I would like to do, but suddenly nothing seems urgent. Maybe it would be fun to play hockey with Dad and Ethan. "Sure," I say, turning around to face them. "Why not?"

chapter thirteen

Even though it's November, Monday morning feels like spring. The warm, sunny weather has put everyone in a good mood. Kids stream into the school, laughing and talking to their friends. Even I'm feeling better today. Last night, I finally told my dad the whole story. I could tell he was worried, but at least he didn't give me a big lecture. And I think it helped just to share the secret with someone besides Daniel.

When I called his house last night, Mrs. Cooper said the doctor had decided to keep Daniel in the hospital for another day. "He's going to be okay," she said, but her voice was serious. "I don't know if he will go back to school this week or not." Still, just hearing that Daniel would recover was great news.

Can I finally put what happened completely behind me? I'm not sure. The police may need to talk to me again, and someday Wendell may decide to settle the score. But, I'm safe for now.

As I head down the hallway toward homeroom, I check my watch. Five minutes until the bell. A few feet away, I can see Travis, standing at his locker, talking to Maya. As soon as I see her, everything else flies out of my head. I brace myself, expecting to get chewed out for deserting her on Friday night. Then I realize she's smiling. She tosses her long hair over her shoulder. "Hi, Shawn," she says sweetly. "You missed an amazing concert this weekend."

"I did?" I take a deep breath and notice she smells good—vaguely like vanilla ice cream—but I refuse to let myself think about it. I have something to tell her. "You know, I'm really sorry about Friday night, Maya. Did I tell you I was grounded?"

"Yeah, I know," she says breezily. "Travis told me. He came to the concert instead."

"Oh, yeah?" I squint suspiciously at Travis. He responds with a shrug.

"It was a good concert, wasn't it, Trav?" she asks.

"Not bad," he says. "I didn't think the lead guitarist was all that good—"

"Anyway," Maya says cutting him off, "they're playing again this Saturday night. Can you make it?" She's looking at me challengingly, like she's daring me to say no.

"Uh, well, sure," I say.

"I mean, if you're not grounded," she adds.

"Right."

Travis is busy watching us like we're

competing at table tennis. I really wish he'd buzz off.

"Hey," Maya says suddenly. "Our group is supposed to be doing a presentation on Friday. Should we be working on it?"

This time, I'm ready for her. "Definitely. We should—you know—talk about it. How about later today? At Coffee World?"

Maya is about to say, "Yes," but before she has time, Ms. Wolischuk wanders out of her classroom and looks around. "I need someone to give me a hand with some boxes," she announces. "You'll do, Travis," she says pointing at him. Then her eyes rest on me. "Shawn," she says, she's frowning slightly, "don't you owe me a chemistry test?"

"Yes," I mumble. "I'm really sorry—" I'm about to apologize for not turning up last week, but Ms. Wolischuk cuts me off.

"No excuses, please. Really, this has gone on long enough. I was away with the flu last week, but I'm all ready for you now. You can write the test after school today."

"Today?" I ask.

"Today," she says firmly. "There is no time like the present. You've had lots of opportunity to study. I'll see you at four." And with that, she sweeps back into her classroom.

"Sure." I look over at Maya apologetically. What can I do? How can I meet her after school now? I expect her to be annoyed, but instead she looks like she's ready to laugh.

"Hey, don't worry about it," she says with a shrug. "There's always tomorrow!"

Diane Young is a writer and editor who lives in Toronto, Canada. When she was a child, she used to create illustrated books that she sold to her friends for a quarter. When she grew up, becoming an editor seemed like the most natural thing in the world. After working on many novels for children and adults, she decided that it was finally time to write something herself. *See No Evil* is her debut.

Other titles in the Orca Currents series

Visit www.orcabook.com for more information.